Dotty on the Potty

Dotty on the Potty

Written by Claudia Merandi

Illustrations by Stephanie Gibadlo

JEBWizard Publishing

Copyright 2019 by Claudia Merandi

All rights reserved.

ISBN: 978-1-7335264-7-0

Hi! My name is Dotty!

I'm nine years old, and I live in Pottytown, USA. I live with my mommy, my daddy, and my big brother, Toddy.

I go to a really nice school with really nice friends. I get to wear a pretty uniform every day.

My best friends are Arty and Marty

I love school, but sometimes my tummy hurts when I eat lunch.

When my tummy hurts, I can't play with the other kids at recess. I feel sad when that happens.

Arty and Marty help me feel better because they know I have a bad tummy problem.

When I was six, my mommy noticed I wasn't growing.

I had to go to a special doctor, a doctor that knows all about bad tummies.

I really like my doctor. His name is Dr. Smarty. He has the best toys to play with in his office.

Dr. Smarty told me I would need a special test. Dr. Smarty put a tube in me to see inside of my tummy. That's when he told my mommy I had Crohn's Disease.

He told me with medication, my tummy would feel better. I also had to stop eating certain foods. My tummy doesn't like certain foods.

Dr. Smarty told me I would have to take the medicine. It was a special medicine that I would get at the children's hospital, and I would have to get an IV put in my arm. That sounded scary!

But once I went to the children's hospital, I met all really nice boys and girls who had a sad tummy just like mine. I felt happy to meet other kids who had what I had.

My nurse is really nice! His name is Barney.

He has me hold my breath and then he puts a little needle into my arm.

My special medicine is called Remicade.

It takes about three hours for the special medicine to get into my body.

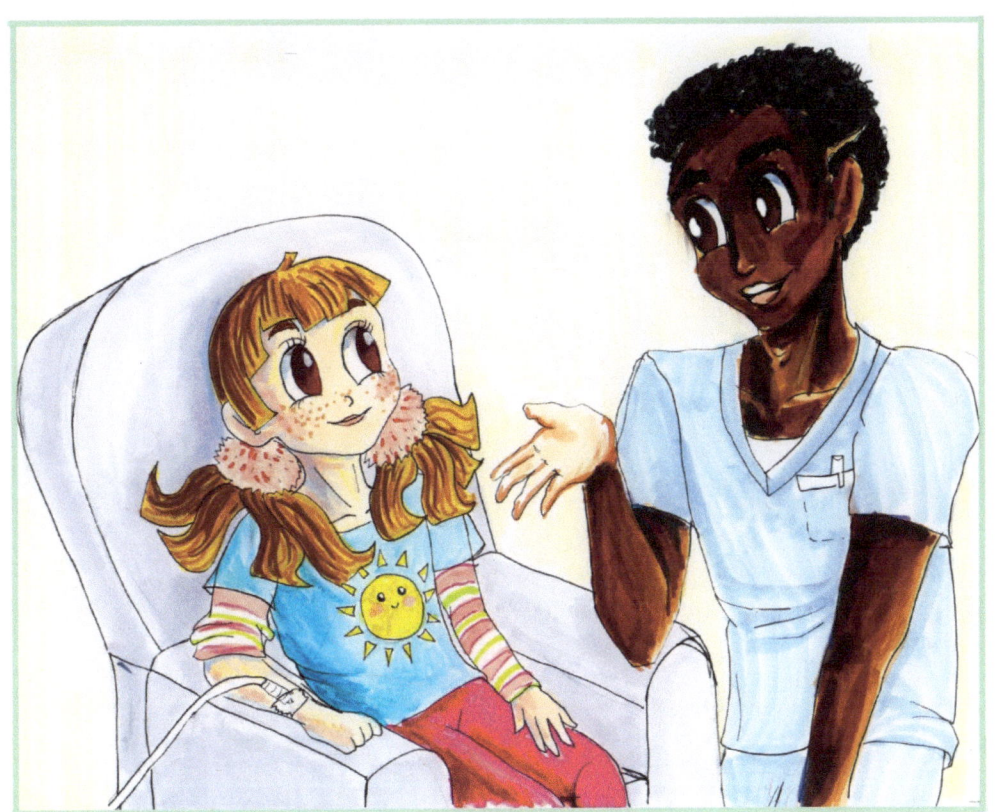

It's nice to know I'm not the only little girl with a bad tummy.

While I'm getting my medicine, I sit and watch movies with the other kids.

Some kids have Colitis and some have Crohn's Disease.

After my medicine is done, I get tired. So, when I go home, I usually take a nap.

When I wake up, if I feel good, I will play hide and seek with my brother, Toddy.

Sometimes my medicine doesn't work, and I get really bad tummy aches. I have to stay in the hospital. I get sad when this happens, but it's a hospital for kids so there is always fun stuff to do!

My brother, Toddy, will stay with me and watch TV after he gets out of school. And when Toddy is there with me, he can eat all the ice cream he wants. There is a refrigerator that has ice cream, Jello, popsicles, and different kinds of cookies.

When my tummy hurts, I don't like to eat, but I don't mind if Toddy does.

I'm really lucky that I have nice doctors and nurses to help me when I'm in the hospital.

I do get sad sometimes in the hospital, but I feel better when my mommy, daddy, and brother come to visit me.

I'm glad that I have really nice doctors and nurses that can help me when my tummy hurts, and I'm glad I have my special medication.

Sometimes I do get sad and cry, but then I feel better the next day.

My mommy always says,

"What a difference a day makes."

If you have Crohn's Disease or any other kind of bad tummy, don't be sad. Don't be afraid because your doctor will be able to help you with your special medicine.

If you have Crohn's, tell your friends. It will make you feel better and you won't be embarrassed if you have to go to the potty a lot like I do.

I hope you liked my story!

About the Author

Claudia Merandi, 50, of East Providence, RI has struggled with Crohn's Disease since she was a child. 'She's been on maintenance therapy, consisting of monthly Remicade infusions along with weekly Methotrexate injections.
Claudia wrote "Dotty on the Potty" shortly after publishing her first book, "*Crohn's Disease, the other 'C' word: Crohn's Disease, Court Reporting, and Custody Battles.*"
(Amazon)
Claudia, a fitness competitor, raises money for Cure For IBD.
"The goal of this book is to bring a smile to a little girl who is battling Crohn's or any other form of IBD/IBS/Colitis."
"*Lewy on the Loo,*" the little boy's version, is in development for 2020.

Illustrator

Stephanie Gibadlo is an artist who desires to bring joy to others through her artwork.

She is a graduate of the Rhode Island School of Design. Her favorite things to draw are all types of people and birds (with a particular fondness for pigeons). You can find more of her work on her website, stephaniegibadlo.com, and her instagram @stephaniegibadlo"

Proceeds from "Dotty on the Potty" will benefit Cure For IBD, a foundation that focuses on research for little ones with stomach-related issues.

www.ingramcontent.com/pod-product-compliance
Lightning Source LLC
Chambersburg PA
CBHW040301100526

44584CB00004BA/296